THE UNITED STATES: PAST AND PRESENT™

FEB 2011

NEW YORK

Past and Present

J. Elizabeth Mills

New York

NORTHPORT PUBLIC LIBRARY
NORTHPORT, NEW YORK

To Uncle Ted—from your cabin in Chateaugay to hikes at Ausable Chasm, the North Country will stay with me always

Published in 2010 by The Rosen Publishing Group, Inc.
29 East 21st Street, New York, NY 10010

Copyright © 2010 by The Rosen Publishing Group, Inc.

First Edition

All rights reserved. No part of this book may be reproduced in any form without permission in writing from the publisher, except by a reviewer.

Library of Congress Cataloging-in-Publication Data

Mills, J. Elizabeth.
New York: past and present / J. Elizabeth Mills.—1st ed.
   p. cm.—(The United States: past and present)
Includes bibliographical references and index.
ISBN-13: 978-1-4358-5285-3 (library binding)
ISBN-13: 978-1-4358-5568-7 (pbk)
ISBN-13: 978-1-4358-5569-4 (6 pack)
1. New York (State)—Juvenile literature. I. Title.
F119.3.M55 2010
974.7—dc22

2008054256

Manufactured in the United States of America

On the cover: Top left: The Statue of Liberty, located in New York Harbor, has greeted immigrants to the United States for more than a century. Top right: The trading floor of the New York Stock Exchange bustles with activity. Bottom: Niagara Falls attracts tourists from all over the world.

Contents

Introduction	5
Chapter 1 **The Land of New York**	6
Chapter 2 **The History of New York**	13
Chapter 3 **The Government of New York**	21
Chapter 4 **The Economy of New York**	26
Chapter 5 **People from New York: Past and Present**	31
Timeline	37
New York at a Glance	38
Glossary	40
For More Information	41
For Further Reading	43
Bibliography	43
Index	46

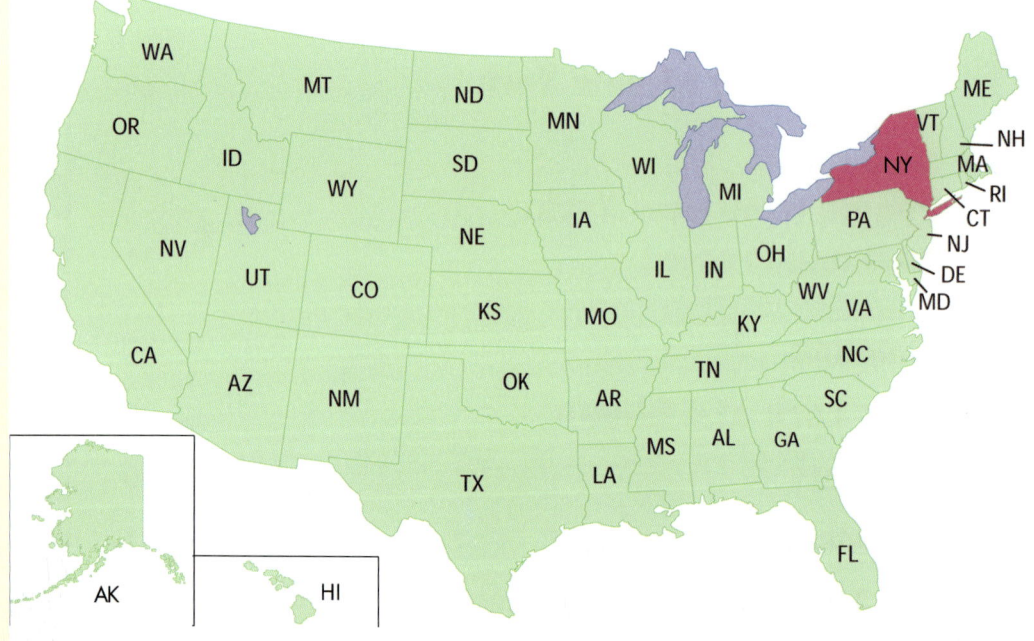

Top: Mountains and lakes are found in and around the state of New York. Bottom: New York is located in the northeastern region of the United States.

4

Introduction

What comes to mind when you think of New York? Bright lights? Tall buildings? Crowded streets? The smell of hot dogs and gasoline? Then you're thinking of New York City, one of the largest and best-known cities in the world. But there is much more to the state of New York than just its biggest city.

New York State is often thought to be split between two very different lifestyles and geographical settings. The New York City area is a cosmopolitan center full of theater, concerts, sporting events, and a vast array of restaurants. It is almost entirely urban, with the exception of Long Island, which has a distinct farming and fishing community.

Upstate New York, on the other hand, has farms and barns and miles of open countryside. There are also some big cities in Upstate New York, particularly Buffalo—the second-largest city in the state. Most of New York's farming and agricultural industries are located in this region.

New York State is full of variety in its people, its economy, and its landscape. There are so many things to see and do in this one-of-a-kind Northeastern state.

Chapter 1

The Land of NEW YORK

New York is nestled between quiet New England peaks and bustling Mid-Atlantic waterways. It is bordered by Canada, New Jersey, Pennsylvania, Massachusetts, Vermont, and Connecticut. Long ago, during an ice age, massive glaciers moved across this land. These hulks of ice and snow sculpted low valleys and smoothed jagged peaks, creating a diverse landscape of plateaus, lowlands, coastal plains, and mountainous regions.

The North Country

Imagine you're standing on the summit of Mt. Marcy—the highest peak in the Adirondack mountain range and the highest point in New York. Forests stretch as far as you can see. This area is a popular place for hikers. Take a deep breath and breathe in good, clean air. You are standing in the biggest national park in the continental United States. These rounded mountains cover about a quarter of the state. Mt. Marcy's summit has a small lake called Lake Tear of the Clouds. This lake is the source of the Hudson River. From here, the Hudson travels more than 300 miles (482 kilometers) south to the Atlantic Ocean.

The Land of New York

In 1901, Theodore Roosevelt made camp on the summit of Mt. Marcy—5,344 feet (1,629 meters) above sea level.

South of the Adirondacks are the Hudson Highlands and the Taconic Mountains. The Taconic peaks form part of the border between New York and Connecticut, Massachusetts, and Vermont.

The Lowlands

The lowlands of New York have some of the most fertile farmlands in the state. When the glaciers melted, they left behind mineral-rich soil that is perfect for growing crops. This region includes Hudson

NEW YORK: Past and Present

The Environment

Did you know that at one point, between five hundred and three hundred million years ago, New York State was under water? Scientists know this because of the kinds of rock that were left behind when the seas dried up. There were also volcanoes and barren, cold, flat plains. Wooly mammoths and arctic foxes roamed about. But then the climate warmed, and people arrived and began to build. Huts became shacks, and these shacks became cabins. Cabins turned into more complex buildings and then skyscrapers. All of this construction and all of the people who have come to live in this area have damaged the environment greatly.

New York's air and water are badly polluted. Gasoline fumes dirty the air, and dumped waste turns the water toxic. Garbage is perhaps New York's biggest problem. New Yorkers dispose of 23 million tons (23,000,000,000 kilograms) of waste every year, and the city is no longer able to dump this waste into landfills. New York has started to ship the waste to other states. But the city's trash alone requires a line of trucks several miles long.

The state has started to find solutions to these problems. The New York Department of Environmental Conservation oversees and protects the state's natural resources as well as public health and safety. This has led to cleaner air and water and the closing of many landfills. New York continues to find new ways to protect its resources and improve its climate, making it a better place for everyone.

Valley and Mohawk Valley, the Great Lakes Plain, and the St. Lawrence Valley.

The Hudson Valley includes the area north of New York City and around Lake George and Lake Champlain. The Mohawk Valley sits between the Adirondacks and the Appalachian Plateau. It provides transportation from the Atlantic Ocean through the Appalachian

Mountains. The gentle hills and flat land of the Great Lakes Plain are situated between Lake Erie and Lake Ontario.

The St. Lawrence Valley starts at Lake Ontario and heads northeast with the St. Lawrence River. At 744 miles (1,197 km) long, the St. Lawrence River is even longer than the Hudson River. It is part of the international boundary between the United States and Canada. Niagara Falls is also located here, on the Niagara River between Canada and New York. Niagara Falls is an extremely popular tourist destination. It has three different waterfalls: Horseshoe Falls, American Falls, and Bridal Veil Falls.

Appalachian Plateau

The Appalachian Plateau is the biggest land region in the state, with six major rivers flowing through it. Here, the rough Catskill Mountains loom out over the surrounding region at elevations of 3,000 to 4,000 feet (914 to 1,219 m). The Catskills consist of more than thirty peaks. The Delaware River flows from the Catskills to form a portion of New York's border with Pennsylvania, and it provides much of New York City's water supply. Other mountain ranges in the area include the Shawangunk and the Allegheny mountains.

This region has various kinds of farms and vineyards near the Finger Lakes and the Catskills.

Atlantic Coastal Plain

This flat plain starts in Massachusetts, includes Long Island and Staten Island, and travels along the Atlantic coast to Florida. Sandy beaches and fruit and vegetable farms can be found out on Long Island.

NEW YORK: *Past and Present*

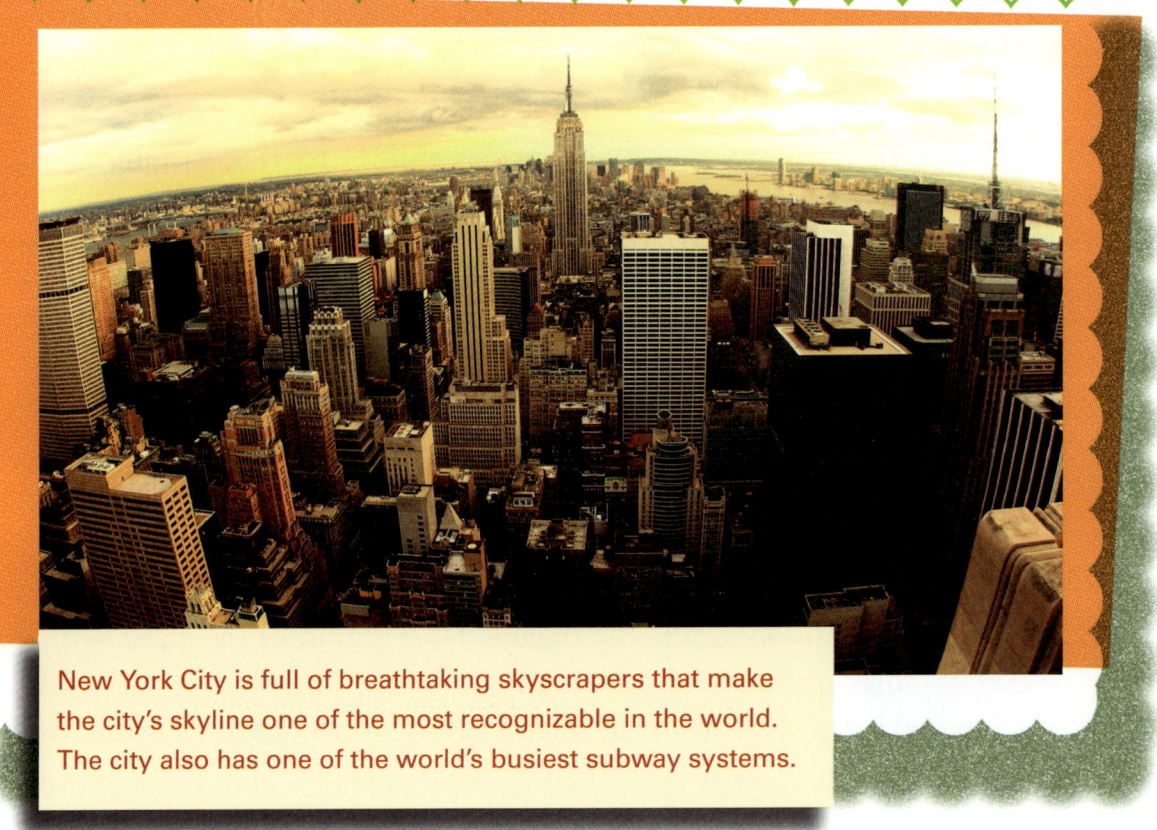

New York City is full of breathtaking skyscrapers that make the city's skyline one of the most recognizable in the world. The city also has one of the world's busiest subway systems.

New York City and the Five Boroughs

Traveling down to New York City, we come to the most populated city in the country. It is home of the Brooklyn Bridge, the Empire State Building, the Chrysler Building, the United Nations, Central Park, the Statue of Liberty, and the Bronx Zoo. The landscape here has skyscrapers instead of mountains, fountains instead of lakes, and five unique boroughs: Manhattan, Brooklyn, Queens, the Bronx, and Staten Island.

The Land of New York

Climate

New York's climate is as varied as its food and its people. Four distinct seasons punctuate the year, with weather extremes in winter and summer.

Towns in Upstate New York, such as Buffalo, Rochester, and Syracuse, get heaps of snow in the winter. Snow also falls in the Catskills and the Adirondacks, making them popular destinations for winter sports like skiing. Lake Placid, in the North Country, is home to Whiteface Mountain, a big ski resort. The Winter Olympics were held there twice.

Closer to New York City, the temperatures are somewhat milder. However, the winters are still cold. Ocean breezes moderate the weather and climate in the five boroughs. Average temperatures in January can vary from 33 degrees Fahrenheit (0.5 degrees Celsius) on Long Island to 14°F (10°C) in the Adirondack mountain range.

In the spring, melting snow and rain fill the rivers and lakes to the brim, and flowers bloom in every color throughout the state. Summers heat up in New York City, even near the ocean, and are often very humid. But temperatures in the mountains stay brisk and cool.

Plants and Animals

Many plants and animals live in New York, mostly upstate. In fact, New York is home to 103 different kinds of mammals. Many of these animals live all over the state, such as the white-footed mouse, gray squirrel, skunk, raccoon, groundhog, and white-tailed deer. Other animals are local to certain areas, such as beavers—the beaver is the state animal of New York. Black bears live in the dense forests. And moose and

NEW YORK: *Past and Present*

Hundreds of deer roam all over Fire Island National Seashore, on Long Island. They eat several pounds of plants every day.

coyotes prefer the cool North Country. New York's skies are full of more than three hundred species of birds, from those that stay all year long like the pigeons and crows, and those that arrive for certain seasons, such as Canada geese and robins. The state's rivers are teeming with several kinds of fish, from trout to salmon, bass to perch, and more.

Forests of birch, ash, pine, and maple cover the hills in waves of green. Maple trees are especially important to New York. In the early part of the year, during the months of February and March, farmers tap into maple trees and collect sap. They boil the sap in huge vats and turn it into maple syrup for pancakes, waffles, and candy.

Chapter 2

The History of New York

When North America was still covered in glaciers, about fifteen thousand to thirty-five thousand years ago, a group of ancient peoples called Paleo-Indians traveled over a land bridge between North America and Asia. They hunted mammoths, mastodons, and other big animals for food, clothing, and shelter. They became the first settlers in the land that would later become New York. The descendants of the Paleo-Indians were the Algonquin and the Iroquois tribes.

European Settlers

European explorers began arriving in North America in the 1500s, including Giovanni da Verrazano, who was the first European to see New York. These men were looking for a direct route to Asia as a way to increase trade. In 1603, a man named Samuel de Champlain traveled from France to Canada to trade furs with the native peoples. In 1609, he claimed the northern region of New York as French territory, including a lake that would bear his name.

Also that year, an English explorer named Henry Hudson helped the Dutch set up trading posts along the river that bears his name. Furs were traded for guns, blankets, and other goods. The success of these trades enabled the Dutch to set up two colonies: Fort Orange

NEW YORK: Past and Present

Henry Hudson sailed the ship *Half Moon* first to Nova Scotia and then to the river that was named for him.

and New Amsterdam. The first European settlers in these colonies were Dutch, but then people began to arrive from all over Europe, speaking many different languages. The colonies grew, and by the 1660s, there were more than nine thousand people living in New Amsterdam.

These colonies wouldn't stay under Dutch control for long. The English had already settled in Massachusetts and Connecticut, and they were looking to acquire new colonies. In 1664, British warships took New Amsterdam from its governor, Peter Stuyvesant, and renamed it New York, for the Duke of York. They seized Long Island and changed the name of Fort Orange to Albany. British territory now stretched across New York, New Jersey, and Vermont, as well as part of Connecticut.

Wars

Britain's win in the French and Indian War gave them control over New York. But the British government needed money to pay for the war. They decided to tax goods that were bought by the colonies. The colonists, however, disagreed and began to revolt. Their protests led to the Revolutionary War, much of which was fought in New York. General George Washington led his troops through New York

The History of New York

City and Upstate New York, fighting battles along the way. New York City was under British rule until the war ended in 1783.

On July 26, 1788, New York entered the Union as the eleventh state. George Washington was sworn in as the first president of the United States in an inaugural ceremony that took place in New York City. The city was the nation's capital from 1785 to 1790.

The Iroquois Confederacy was made up of six tribes from what would become the state of New York: the Mohawk, the Oneida, the Onondaga, the Cayuga, and the Seneca. All, except the Oneida, had sided with the British during the Revolutionary War and attacked American settlements. The end of the war resulted in many tribes moving to Canada or being forced onto reservations.

New York played a lesser role in the War of 1812, hosting just two naval battles. But the British were defeated in both, which took place on Lake Erie and Lake Champlain.

George Washington was greeted and celebrated all along his journey to New York City for his inauguration ceremony.

15

Industrial New York

After the war, some people moved up into the wilderness of western New York. Others stayed in New York City. They laid out roads and railways and built steamships. They constructed the Erie Canal.

New York City became one of the busiest ports in the world, handling all kinds of goods. Tall buildings shot up in the city. New industries developed, such as newspapers, banking, shipbuilding, and others. Factories were churning out products and creating new jobs. By the mid-1800s, New York's population had swelled to three million people. Immigrants arrived constantly from Ireland and Germany.

Slavery

Not all people came to New York on their own free will. A group of powerful Dutch merchants formed the Dutch West India Company, and they brought slaves from Africa to New York in the 1600s. By the end of the eighteenth century, there were more than twenty thousand slaves in New York. These slaves cleared forests for roads, built buildings, and worked on farms. Though the slave trade was banned in 1788, the laws still allowed certain forms of slavery to continue. Slavery was officially abolished in the state in 1827. Former slaves were given the right to vote in 1870 with the Fifteenth Amendment to the Constitution.

Civil War

The country began to divide over the issue of slavery. The Northern states wanted to end slavery altogether. The Southern states felt that each state should be able to decide whether or not to allow slaves. This disagreement escalated into the Civil War, which lasted from

The History of New York

1861 to 1865. New Yorkers were brought into the Union army to fight for the North, but they could avoid the war by paying $300. Those who could not afford such a luxury protested, and they worried that freed slaves would head north and compete with them for jobs. A riot broke out in New York City. The riot became known as the Draft Riots and lasted for three days. But in the end, New York sent the most soldiers of any other state—more than 460,000—and provided the most money and supplies. The North won the war in 1865.

The Gilded Age

In the aftermath of the Civil War, New York entered a period known as the Gilded Age. Factories churned out products like iron, steel, clothing, and electrical equipment. Such production contributed to the great prosperity of the city. Pennsylvania Station and Grand Central Depot were constructed. Men including John D. Rockefeller, Cornelius Vanderbilt, and John Pierpont Morgan became millionaires from the success of these industries. The huge homes and rich lifestyles of these giants contrasted harshly with the

Cornelius Vanderbilt bought land for the first Grand Central Depot in 1869. It was later renovated into today's Grand Central Station.

17

struggles and suffering of the immigrants who arrived by the boatload every day at Ellis Island, greeted by the Statue of Liberty.

Hundreds of thousands of people—primarily from eastern Europe, Italy, and Ireland—found jobs in factories. They often worked seven days a week, despite the dangerous and low-paid jobs that they were given. Many immigrants lived in filthy and overcrowded tenement housing that was located in rough neighborhoods. And yet, many immigrants were able to make a living and eventually make a better life for themselves.

In 1883, the Brooklyn Bridge was opened, and people spread out into Brooklyn. In 1898, the five boroughs of New York City became one unified city.

Tammany Hall

Amidst all of this expansion and growth, a political community was developing in New York City called Tammany Hall. Tammany Hall was a Democratic Party organization. It began in 1789 as an opposition to the Republican upper class who had been in power since the American Revolution. Tammany Hall's leaders were picked from among Irish immigrants. They helped other immigrants find work and gain citizenship. In return, people continued to vote for Tammany Hall. Not all leaders of Tammany Hall were good, however. William Marcy "Boss" Tweed stole money from the government and lived quite a rich lifestyle despite his small income. Tweed was at last found guilty and sent to jail, where he died in 1878. One man who tried to undo the damage done by Boss Tweed was Theodore Roosevelt, a young police commissioner. But Tammany Hall remained powerful for many years.

The History of New York

Transportation

Did you know that in 1900, there were about 130,000 horses working in Manhattan? They pulled people in wagons, turned huge cranks that powered machines, pulled steam fire engines, and hauled streetcars. Think of all the taxicabs in Manhattan today. The number of horses in the city in the early twentieth century outnumbered today's cabs ten to one!

The horses that pulled steam engines were in top form. The engines were heavy, so the horses had to be strong. The fire alarm could ring at any hour of the day or night, so the horses had to be quick and alert. And the horses had to stay calm while firefighters sprayed water onto burning buildings.

Twentieth-Century New York

New York's good fortune would not last long. People were spending too much money and were not earning enough in their jobs. Factories were manufacturing more products than people could buy. The stock market was handling billions of dollars every day. Then, on October 29, 1929, a day that would later be called Black Tuesday, the stock market crashed. Millions of people lost all of their savings. This was the start of the Great Depression. People stood in long lines for food, and children were put to work to try and earn anything that they could.

Theodore Roosevelt's cousin, Franklin Delano Roosevelt, became New York's governor in 1929. He created many social programs to help his state get back on its feet. When he became president of the United States in 1933, Franklin Roosevelt expanded these programs to help the entire nation, creating jobs and welfare programs for those in need.

NEW YORK: Past and Present

During the Great Depression, breadlines and soup kitchens were often the only sources of free food for thousands of starving, unemployed people.

The Future of New York

On September 11, 2001, a terrible event happened. Terrorists captured commercial jet planes and flew two of them into the World Trade Center towers in New York City. These twin towers represented the country's commercial success, and they stood out against the city's unique skyline. But that morning, they tumbled to the ground and nearly three thousand people died. Other planes were hijacked and crashed that morning—one at the Pentagon in Arlington, Virginia, and the other in a field in Pennsylvania. New Yorkers were both stunned and saddened by this tragedy. But little by little, they pulled themselves up again and kept living, working, and carrying on the spirit of New York.

Chapter 3

The Government of New York

New York's government is built upon its constitution. The document was drawn up and adopted in 1797, before New York became a state. New York was the first of the original thirteen colonies to have its own constitution. Voters can decide to change the document every twenty years. New constitutions were adopted in 1821, 1846, and 1894.

State Capital

The capital of New York is Albany, a town in Upstate New York that was originally called Fort Orange. A state's capital is the place where the capitol building is located. Government officials work at the capitol building and make laws.

The capitol building in Albany was completed in 1899 after thirty-two years of construction. It cost about $25 million, making it the most expensive building in the nation at the time. The building is beautiful, with its fancy staircases and impressive size. The capitol flies the state flag, which was adopted in 1901.

New York City was originally the state capital until 1797, when the capital was relocated to Albany. New York City was also the nation's capital from 1785 to 1790.

NEW YORK: Past and Present

In 1911, the capitol building of New York was almost destroyed by a terrible fire. Unusual materials used to build the Assembly Chamber kept the fire from spreading too far.

Branches of New York State Government

The New York State government is split into three branches, or sections: executive, legislative, and judicial. These branches work together to pass and enforce laws for the people of New York.

Executive Branch

The executive branch makes sure that the laws of New York State are being obeyed. The head of the executive branch is the governor. The governor is elected by the people of New York for a term of four years. At the end of that term, the governor must prove that he or she is worthy of being re-elected in a campaign. Otherwise, the governor must give up the seat to someone new. The governor appoints,

The Government of New York

or hires, judges and department heads; prepares the budget, which shows how the state's money will be spent over the following year; and accepts or vetoes laws. A veto is a rejection of a proposed law. The governor holds a powerful position. Four governors have gone on to become U.S. presidents: Martin Van Buren, Grover Cleveland, Theodore Roosevelt, and Franklin Delano Roosevelt.

Several people help the governor. The lieutenant governor, attorney general, and comptroller are elected to four-year terms as well.

As police commissioner, Theodore Roosevelt authorized a bike squad of policemen who caught speeding cyclists and motorists.

Legislative Branch

The legislative branch makes the laws. There are two houses in New York State: the Assembly and the Senate. The Senate has sixty-two members, and the Assembly has 150. These members are called legislators, and they are elected for two-year terms by their local districts. The head of the Assembly is the Speaker, who is elected by the members of the Assembly for a two-year term. The head of the Senate is the Senate majority leader, who is elected for a two-year term by members of the Senate.

The legislature focuses on making laws on how to use state money for government agencies, how to determine if something is a crime

NEW YORK: Past and Present

Elections

Did you know that people used to vote in elections using colored beans or corn kernels? In colonial America, elections were held very differently than they are today. An election is a process that allows citizens to choose leaders, such as mayors or presidents.

In colonial times, people running for office could stand right next to the people counting votes and see how they were doing in the race. Secrecy was not an important part of elections at that time.

In the mid-1900s, some political parties created their own ballots listing only the names of their candidates. Voters could simply drop that ballot into the box, regardless of whether the names were readable or recognizable.

In an effort to avoid election fraud, a man named Jacob H. Myers invented a mechanical lever vote counter that needed no paper at all. It first appeared in Rochester, New York, in 1892. By the middle of the twentieth century, these machines were used across the country. But the machines eventually broke down and could no longer be reliable.

Today, votes are cast in secret. Some voters fill out a preprinted piece of paper called a ballot or use electronic voting machines.

and what sort of punishment it deserves, protecting and caring for people through programs like welfare, and amending or correcting an old law.

A proposed law is called a bill. Any member of the Senate or Assembly can create a bill. The bill must be approved by most of the members, or a majority, of both houses. Then, the bill is sent to the governor for his or her signature or veto. If the governor signs the bill, it becomes a law. However, if the governor vetoes the bill, it can still become a law, but only if two-thirds of the members in both houses decide to overturn the veto.

Judicial Branch

The judicial branch explains the laws that have been passed and enforced by the other two branches of government. The judicial branch is made up of the New York court system.

The dome at the Court of Appeals has a mural that is 1,000 feet (304 m) long and 34 feet (10 m) wide.

New York's court system has many levels. The highest court is the Court of Appeals. This court is made up of six associate judges and one chief judge who are appointed by the governor for terms of fourteen years. These judges review decisions made by lower courts to determine if the decisions were fair and legal.

The next court is the Supreme Court, which is separated into twelve judicial districts. This court has twelve justices who are elected for fourteen-year terms. The Supreme Court hears original cases and reviews appeals.

Below the Supreme Court is the claims court, and then each county has its own family court and surrogate court. Family courts hear cases regarding minors—children under the age of eighteen—and family-related issues. Surrogate courts deal with the wills and estates of people who have died. County courts also hear civil and criminal cases.

Chapter 4

The Economy of New York

Where do New Yorkers work? Historically, they've worked mostly in the manufacturing sector, making goods in factories. Recently, though, more New Yorkers work in service-related industries like banking, real estate, insurance, restaurants, and others. Manufacturing is still a part of the state's economy, but it employs fewer people than before.

New York City is the heart of commerce in the state. Most New Yorkers live in New York City, and their jobs account for most of the money that goes to the state. The majority of the jobs in New York City are service-related, with banking, finance, communication, advertising, and tourism as the top industries. New York is the home of the New York Stock Exchange, the American Stock Exchange, and several major media companies, including Hearst Corporation, Time Warner, and Viacom. Three major television networks have their headquarters in the city: ABC, CBS, and NBC.

Manufacturing and Service Industries

New York City's top manufacturing industries include clothing, electronic equipment, and printed materials like books, magazines, and newspapers.

The Economy of New York

The garment, or clothing, industry started in the nineteenth century, when hundreds of immigrants worked in clothing shops. At the time, these shops were mostly located down on the Lower East Side. Now, they have spread to Chinatown in Manhattan and to Sunset Park in Brooklyn, and Flushing in Queens. The city's publishing business dates back to the publication of its first newspaper, the *New York Gazette*, in 1725. The current papers in New York City are the *New York Times*, the *New York Post*, the *Wall Street Journal*, and the *New York Daily News*. Various media companies own many of the major magazines, including *Time*, *Newsweek*, *Sports Illustrated*, and others.

In 1904, the *New York Times* was moved from Nassau Street in Lower Manhattan to 42nd Street, giving the neighborhood the name Times Square.

Long Island offers both service and manufacturing jobs. Some people work in doctor's offices, schools, and hospitals. Others work in factories that make medical technology and high-tech software. Still others work on farms growing fruits and vegetables to sell in the markets of New York City. There is also a modest commercial fishing industry off the Atlantic coast of Long Island.

Farther upstate, Rochester is home to the Eastman Kodak Company, which manufactures cameras and other photographic equipment.

NEW YORK: Past and Present

Tourism

Did you know that, in the nineteenth century, tourism was not a major source of revenue for New York City? But with advancements in transportation, it became easier to travel. Steamships arrived in the harbor and were filled with crowds of people ready to see the city. Though New York City was not initially interested in promoting itself as a tourist destination, tours were readily available by electric bus and boat. The year that the Empire State Building opened, one million people rode its elevator to the top for $1 each. Nowadays, it costs more than $18 to travel to the top! In 1935, the city created the New York Convention and Visitors Bureau to increase its tourism. By the middle of the twentieth century, the bureau had done its job. Eventually, tourism had become a major source of revenue for the city, which is considered one of the top tourist destinations. Tourists were able to travel around the island of Manhattan on tours given by Circle Line, a company that is still around today and has carried more than sixty million passengers since its start in 1945. There are all kinds of historic sites and natural wonders all over the state that attract tourists every year. Niagara Falls draws several million tourists every year, and winter sports enthusiasts gather at Lake Placid. In 2008, the New York Statewide Cultural Tourism Coalition found that New York's tourism industry brings in more than $5.2 billion per year in revenue for state and local governments. That is a pretty good sum for a state that didn't think tourism was very important!

In 1945, Circle Line Cruises started its first sightseeing trip around Manhattan and charged $1.25.

The Economy of New York

Factories in Corning make fiber-optic wires that are used for telecommunications. Albany is a government town full of service jobs. One out of every five people works for the state at the capitol building. Buffalo sits on the Erie Canal. It became New York's second-largest city through the manufacturing and shipping of grain along the canal, as well as railroads and steel. Recently, the city became known for its auto manufacturing and farming.

Across the five boroughs there are twenty-eight open-air farmer's markets that sell fruit and vegetables, baked goods, jams, and many other products.

Agriculture

Even in this high-tech age, farming is still a big industry in New York State. There are more than thirty thousand farms that stretch across a quarter of the land. About a third of New York's income comes from its crops.

New York is a leading producer of apples, maple syrup, grapes, wine, strawberries, cherries, sweet corn, hay, oats, and many other crops. Farmers on livestock farms raise pigs, sheep, and cattle. Vegetable farms, orchards, and vineyards can be found near Lake Erie, along the Finger Lakes, and in the Hudson Valley. In these areas, temperatures stay moderate and the soil is rich with minerals, making it perfect for farming. New York's dairy farms are located in the central and northern parts of the state. New York is one of the leading dairy producers in the country, with more than half of its farm income coming from dairy.

The state's agricultural industry was greatly improved by the opening of the Erie Canal. Farms in the East and in the Midwest were finally connected, and products could be easily transported from one region to the other.

New York and the World

New York's strong economy reaches around the world. This state exports products to more than two hundred countries, including Japan, Israel, Switzerland, Canada, and Mexico. Among the exported goods are electronic equipment, computers, chemicals, crops, minerals, and other natural resources.

In addition, companies from foreign countries have opened offices in New York, investing their money and resources in the state. There are more than three thousand foreign-owned businesses in New York, specifically in fields like sales, finance, banking, and transportation.

Chapter 5

People from New York: Past and Present

New York's vibrant personality and busy pace are reflected in its citizens. The ones listed in this chapter are just a few of the vast array of people who have called New York home.

Susan B. Anthony (1820–1906) Susan Brownell Anthony was born on February 15, 1820, in Adams, Massachusetts. Her family later moved to New York. Anthony dedicated herself first to the temperance movement, an early feminist movement aimed at women and children who were abused by alcoholic husbands and fathers. She also worked tirelessly to give women the right to vote. Though Anthony did not live to see it, the Nineteenth Amendment was ratified on August 18, 1920, making it illegal to deny any citizen the right to vote based on sex. Anthony was also commemorated on the $1 coin.

Ruth Bader Ginsburg (1933–) Ruth Joan Bader was born on March 15, 1933, in Brooklyn, New York. She is an associate justice on the U.S. Supreme Court, appointed by President Bill Clinton in 1993. She was one of only nine women in her class at Harvard Law School in the mid-1950s. She became actively involved with organizations dedicated to civil rights

NEW YORK: Past and Present

Ruth Bader Ginsburg argued cases for women's rights in front of the Supreme Court.

and women's rights. She founded the Women's Rights Project with the American Civil Liberties Union and became the first tenured female professor at Columbia University. She is the first Jewish woman to serve on the U.S. Supreme Court.

Edward Hopper (1882–1967)

Edward Hopper was born on July 22, 1882, in Nyack, New York, along the Hudson River. He decided that he wanted to be an artist while he was still a child, but his parents encouraged him to do illustrations for companies so that he would make more money. He studied art in school and traveled to Europe to see other kinds of artwork. He then traveled all over the United States and Mexico. His paintings depict the people and places that he saw, sometimes in very lonely settings. Hopper's work has been displayed in the Whitney Museum and the Museum of Modern Art, both in New York City.

Michael Jordan (1963–) Michael Jordan was born in Brooklyn, New York, on February 17, 1963. Though he was not very good at basketball initially, he worked hard and developed his signature high leaps and slam dunks. Jordan

People from New York: Past and Present

left school to play for the Chicago Bulls and turned a losing team into a hugely successful one, winning three straight NBA titles. Family tragedy led him to announce an early retirement. He had received three regular-season Most Valuable Player (MVP) awards, three play-off MVP awards, and seven straight scoring titles. He played on the All-Star team every year that he played in the league. Though Jordan was with the Bulls for only nine seasons, he was the team's all-time leading scorer.

Michael Jordan played in the Olympics twice. He's been hailed as one of the greatest basketball players of all time.

Jonas Salk (1914–1995) Jonas Salk was born on October 28, 1914, in New York City to Russian-Jewish immigrant parents. He worked hard in school and became the first person in his family to go to college. He then went to medical school at

NEW YORK: Past and Present

Writers

Did you know that the words "Give me your tired, your poor . . ." were written by a woman named Emma Lazarus in a poem called *The New Colossus*? She wrote the poem in 1883 for an auction intended to raise money for the building of the pedestal of the Statue of Liberty. Unfortunately, her poem was not included in the ceremony, and only five lines of it were included on a plaque placed on the pedestal of the statue after her death.

Many New York writers have written about this incredible state through the centuries. Washington Irving is best known for his short stories, *The Legend of Sleepy Hollow* and *Rip Van Winkle*. But he also wrote *A History of New York*, under the pen name Diedrich Knickerbocker, to poke fun at the early Dutch settlers in Manhattan. James Fenimore Cooper wrote novels like *The Last of the Mohicans* and *The Deerslayer* during the colonial days of eighteenth-century New York, attempting to discuss the mistreatment of Native Americans.

New York University. While he was in medical school, Salk spent a year studying the influenza virus. This research proved to be invaluable later. In the mid-1950s, a crippling disease called poliomyelitis—or polio, for short—was infecting children all over America. Salk devoted himself to finding a cure for this terrible disease. On April 12, 1955, he announced that he had found a cure for polio. Salk was praised and thanked by a grateful country.

Barbra Streisand (1942–) Born Barbara Joan Streisand, Streisand is one of the most successful female entertainers of all time. She has recorded more than sixty albums and sold more than seventy-one million copies of her albums. She has won an Emmy, a Grammy, an Oscar, and a Tony Award, a rare achievement. Streisand was born in Brooklyn to an immigrant father and an American-born mother. She first appeared on television on *The Tonight Show*, in 1961. Her career took off and soon she became a star. She also produced, directed, wrote, and starred in movies including *Yentl*, *The Prince of Tides*, and *The Mirror Has Two Faces*. In 1986, she started the Streisand Foundation, dedicated to supporting many social and political organizations.

Donald Trump (1946–) What New Yorker doesn't recognize the name "Donald Trump"? Whether you know him from his television show *The Apprentice* or from his luxurious hotels, Trump is a larger-than-life figure in New York real estate development. Born on June 14, 1946, in Queens, Trump attended military academy and then business school. He bought land carefully, making sure to pick designs that were attractive and opportunities that would make him lots of money and bring him fame. His buildings are as extravagant as his lifestyle. One skyscraper in Manhattan is decorated in pink marble and actually has an indoor waterfall!

Walt Whitman (1819–1892) Walt Whitman was a printer, teacher, journalist, poet, and above all else, a lover of words. Whitman was born on May 31, 1819. He lived in Brooklyn and on Long Island in the 1820s and 1830s. He founded a newspaper called the *Brooklyn Freeman* and developed a

NEW YORK: *Past and Present*

> Walt Whitman was born in a farmhouse built by his father in 1816. It is now a state historic site.

unique style of poetry. In 1855, Whitman self-published his first volume of poetry, *Leaves of Grass*. A subsequent edition was released in 1856. He traveled to Washington, D.C., to care for his brother, who had been wounded during the Civil War. He stayed there for the next eleven years, working for the hospital. Whitman never had much money, but he did his best to support his family. He published his final volume of poetry in 1891, *Good-Bye My Fancy*.

Timeline

1609	Henry Hudson claims land along the Hudson River for the Dutch; Samuel de Champlain arrives in northern New York and claims the territory for France.
1664	The British take control of New Netherland and rename it New York.
1776	New York colonists declare independence from England.
1788	New York joins the Union as the eleventh state.
1825	The Erie Canal is opened.
1848	The first Women's Rights Convention is held in Seneca Falls.
1888	Blizzard dumps record snowfall on the state.
1925	The *New Yorker* magazine is first published.
1929	The New York Stock Exchange crashes, starting the Great Depression.
1936	*Life* magazine is founded in New York City.
1939–1940	The World's Fair is held in Flushing Meadows.
1952	The United Nations building is completed.
1964–1965	The World's Fair is held in Flushing Meadows.
1973	The World Trade Center towers are dedicated.
1999	The New York Yankees win their twenty-sixth World Series championship.
2001	Terrorists crash two commercial airplanes into the World Trade Center, killing thousands of people.
2009	The New York Yankees and the New York Mets both open new stadiums.

New York at a Glance

State motto	"Excelsior." ("Ever upward.")
State capital	Albany
State flower	Rose
State bird	Bluebird
State tree	Sugar maple
State animal	Beaver
State fruit	Apple
Statehood date and number	July 26, 1788; eleventh state
State nicknames	"The Empire State," "The Knickerbocker State"
Total area and U.S. rank	54,555 square miles (141,297 sq km); twenty-seventh largest state
Population	19,297,729
Length of coastline	127 miles (204 km)
Highest elevation	Mt. Marcy in the Adirondack region, 5,344 feet (1,629 m) above sea level
Lowest elevation	Atlantic coast, sea level

State Flag

State Seal

38

New York at a Glance

Major rivers	St. Lawrence, Hudson, Mohawk, Genesse, Allegheny, Susquehanna, Delaware
Major lakes	Lake Champlain, Lake Ontario, Oneida Lake, Lake Erie, Lake George, Finger Lakes
Hottest temperature recorded	108°F (42°C) in Troy, on July 22, 1926
Coldest temperature recorded	-52°F (-47°C) in Old Forge, on February 18, 1979
Origin of state name	New York was named for the Duke of York in 1664, when the British took New Netherland from the Dutch.
Chief agricultural products	Milk, cheese, maple syrup, apples, grapes, wine, strawberries, cherries, pears, onions, potatoes, cabbage, sweet corn, green beans, cauliflower, field corn, hay, wheat, oats, dry beans
Major industries	Publishing, fashion, pharmaceuticals, machinery, consumer goods, electronics, automotive and aircraft construction

State Bird

State Flower

Glossary

appeal Legal proceeding by which a case is brought before a higher court for review of the decision of a lower court.

ballot A sheet of paper used to cast a secret vote.

capital City where the state government is located.

capitol building Building in which the government meets and carries out its affairs.

climate Weather conditions in a particular location.

economy Management of money being spent.

garment Article of clothing.

glacier Large mass of ice that moves slowly over land.

governor Official elected to act as chief executive of a state.

landfill A method of disposing of trash by burying it between layers of earth to build up low land.

mammoth Extinct relative of the elephant from the Pleistocene era, recognized by its tusks and shaggy hair.

mastodon Extinct relative of the elephant from the Miocene to Pleistocene eras, recognized by its cone-shaped molars.

pedestal The base of an upright structure.

plateau Expanse of flat land raised above nearby land.

ratify To formally approve something.

sap A liquid that flows through a plant.

stock A share, or part, of a company.

stock market Market where stocks are traded.

temperance Moderation.

tenement Low-cost apartment house, often constructed in a poor section of a large city.

tenure Status given to a professional that guarantees employment.

term Length of time that a political official works in an office.

For More Information

Children's Museum of Manhattan
The Tisch Building
212 West 83rd Street
New York, NY 10024
(212) 721-1223
Web site: http://www.cmom.org
The mission of the Children's Museum of Manhattan is to encourage children and their families to learn about themselves and the world around them.

Ellis Island Immigration Museum
Ellis Island
New York, NY 10004
(212) 363-6307
Web site: http://www.ellisisland.org
This museum is located on Ellis Island, in the building where millions of immigrants were processed and allowed entry into the United States.

Lower East Side Tenement Museum
90 Orchard Street
New York, NY 10002
(212) 431-0233
Web site: http://www.tenement.org
Visitors to this museum can see the cramped spaces where many immigrant families lived and learn about some of the people who lived there.

Museum of the City of New York
1220 Fifth Avenue
New York, NY 10029
(212) 534-1672
Web site: http://www.mncy.org
This museum explores the past, present, and future of New York City and celebrates its heritage.

NEW YORK: Past and Present

National Museum of the American Indian
George Gustav Heye Center
One Bowling Green
New York, NY 10004
(212) 514-3700
Web site: http://www.nmai.si.edu
This museum is dedicated to the preservation, study, and exhibition of all aspects of Native American life.

New York City Fire Museum
278 Spring Street
New York, NY 10013
(212) 691-1303, ext. 11
Web site: http://www.nycfiremuseum.org
This museum is located in a former firehouse and has antique engines and equipment, as well as knowledgeable firemen on site to answer questions.

New York Transit Museum
130 Livingston Street, 10th Floor
Brooklyn, NY 11201
(718) 694-1600
Web site: http://www.mta.info
The New York Transit Museum is filled with vintage subway cars, antique turnstiles, and more. It explores the history of transit in New York City.

Web Sites

Due to the changing nature of Internet links, Rosen Publishing has developed an online list of Web sites related to the subject of this book. This site is updated regularly. Please use this link to access this list:

http://www.rosenlinks.com/uspp/nypp

For Further Reading

Bial, Raymond. *Tenement: Immigrant Life on the Lower East Side*. Boston, MA: Houghton Mifflin Co., 2002.

Curlee, Lynn. *Liberty*. New York, NY: Atheneum Books for Young Readers, 2000.

DuTemple, Lesley A. *The New York Subways*. Minneapolis, MN: Lerner Publications Company, 2003.

Kent, Zachary. *The Story of the Brooklyn Bridge*. New York, NY: Children's Press, 1988.

Low, William. *Old Penn Station*. New York, NY: Henry Holt and Co., 2007.

Mann, Elizabeth. *Empire State Building*. New York, NY: Mikaya Press, 2003.

Reynolds, Donald M. *The Architecture of New York City*. New York, NY: John Wiley, 1994.

Bibliography

Academy of Achievement. "Jonas Salk, M.D." February 2, 2005. Retrieved November 25, 2008 (http://www.achievement.org/autodoc/page/sal0bio-1).

Academy of American Poets. "Walt Whitman." Retrieved November 29, 2008 (http://www.poets.org/poet.php/prmPID/126).

Adirondack History. "Out of the Earth: Mining in the Adirondacks." Retrieved November 30, 2008 (http://www.adirondackhistory.org/adkmining/intro.html).

Adirondack History. "Traditional Logging in the Adirondacks." Retrieved November 30, 2008 (http://www.adirondackhistory.org/logging/index.html).

American Museum of Natural History. "The Horse/How We Shaped Horses, How Horses Shaped Us/Heyday of the Horse." Retrieved November 25, 2008 (http://www.amnh.org/exhibitions/horse/?section=howshaped&page=howshaped_c#).

American Museum of Natural History. "The Horse/How We Shaped Horses, How Horses Shaped Us/In the City." Retrieved November 25, 2008 (http://www.amnh.org/exhibitions/horse/?section=howshaped&page=howshaped_ciii).

The Artchive. "Edward Hopper." Retrieved November 28, 2008 (http://www.artchive.com/artchive/H/hopper.html).

Arts & Business Council of New York. "Arts & Business Council of New York and New York State Council on the Arts Announce Support for Nine New York State Cultural

Tourism Projects." June 27, 2007. Retrieved November 29, 2008 (http://www.artsandbusiness-ny.org/news_events/press/2007/003.asp).

Berkey-Gerard, Mark. "New York's Sports Economy." *Gotham Gazette*, March 29, 2004. Retrieved November 28, 2008 (http://www.gothamgazette.com/article/issueoftheweek/20040329/200/933).

City-Data.com. "Buffalo: Economy." Retrieved November 23, 2008 (http://www.city-data.com/us-cities/The-Northeast/Buffalo-Economy.html).

City-Data.com. "New York—Fishing." Retrieved November 30, 2008 (http://www.city-data.com/states/New-York-Fishing.html).

City-Data.com. "New York—Flora and Fauna." Retrieved November 21, 2008 (http://www.city-data.com/states/New-York-Flora-and-fauna.html).

The City of New York. "Biography." Retrieved November 27, 2008 (http://www.nyc.gov/portal/site/nycgov/menuitem.e985cf5219821bc3f7393cd401c789a0).

Cornell University Law School. "Ruth Bader Ginsburg." Retrieved November 26, 2008 (http://www.law.cornell.edu/supct/justices/ginsburg.bio.html).

Cotter, Kristin. *From Sea to Shining Sea: New York*. New York, NY: Children's Press, 2002.

Gardner, Elysa, and Jack Gillum. "Economy Acting Out on Broadway Attendance." *USA Today*, November 18, 2008. Retrieved November 19, 2008 (http://www.usatoday.com/life/theater/news/2008-11-18-broadway-economy_N.htm).

Goodman, Susan E. *On This Spot: An Expedition Back Through Time*. New York, NY: Greenwillow Books, 2004.

Heinrichs, Ann. *America the Beautiful: New York*. New York, NY: Children's Press, 1999.

Homberger, Eric. *The Historical Atlas of New York City*. New York, NY: Henry Holt and Co., 1994 and 2005.

Jackson, Kenneth T., ed. *The Encyclopedia of New York City*. New Haven, CT: Yale University Press, 1995.

Jo-Ki. "Michael Jordan Biography." NotableBiographies.com. Retrieved November 27, 2008 (http://www.notablebiographies.com/Jo-Ki/Jordan-Michael.html).

Litt, Jody. "Susan B. Anthony." University of Rochester. Retrieved November 26, 2008 (http://www.history.rochester.edu/class/sba/first.htm).

Manning, Jason, and Jessica Moore. "2004 Democratic Primaries." PBS Online, *Newshour*, December 15, 2003. Retrieved December 14, 2008 (http://www.pbs.org/newshour/vote2004/primaries/sr_technology_history.html).

McAuliffe, Emily. *New York: Facts and Symbols*. New York, NY: Capstone Press, 1998.

Bibliography

McDonnell, Timothy. "Physical Geography." Geography of New York State. Retrieved November 20, 2008 (http://www.nygeo.org/ny_geo.html).

Microsoft Encarta Online Encyclopedia. "Iroquois." MSN.com, 2008. Retrieved November 24, 2008 (http://encarta.msn.com/encyclopedia_761552484/Iroquois.html).

National Women's Hall of Fame. "Nellie Bly." Women of the Hall. Retrieved November 22, 2008 (http://www.greatwomen.org/women.php?action=viewone&id=23).

New York State Department of Agriculture and Markets. "Commodities." Retrieved November 28, 2008 (http://www.agmkt.state.ny.us/NY_Commodities.html).

New York State Senate. "About the Senate: Branches of Government." Retrieved November 22, 2008 (http://www.senate.state.ny.us/sws/aboutsenate/branches_gov.html#judicial).

North, Douglas. "Slavery in New York." Slavery in the North. Retrieved November 24, 2008 (http://www.slavenorth.com/newyork.htm).

Obringer, Lee Ann. "How Going Over Niagara Works." How Stuff Works. Retrieved November 24, 2008 (http://adventure.howstuffworks.com/niagara1.htm).

PBS Kids. "Big Apple History." Retrieved November 20, 2008 (http://pbskids.org/bigapplehistory/early/index-flash.html).

Photo Seminars. "Margaret Bourke-White." Retrieved November 27, 2008 (http://www.photo-seminars.com/Fame/MargaretWhite.htm).

Sandler, Martin W. *America's Great Disasters*. New York, NY: HarperCollins Children's Books, 2003.

Schomp, Virginia. *Celebrate the States: New York*. New York, NY: Marshall Cavendish, 2006.

Subik, Jason. "State's Farm Rolls Drop Again." *Daily Gazette*, February 5, 2008. Retrieved November 24, 2008 (http://www.dailygazette.com/news/2008/feb/05/0205_farms).

INDEX

A
Adirondacks, 6, 7, 8, 11
Albany, 14, 21, 29
animals, 8, 11–12, 19
Appalachian Plateau, 8, 9

B
Buffalo, 5, 11, 29

C
Catskills, 9, 11
Champlain, Samuel de, 13
Civil War, 16–17
Cleveland, Grover, 23

D
Draft Riots, 17

E
Ellis Island, 18
Empire State Building, 10, 28
Erie Canal, 16, 29, 30
European settlers, 13–14
executive branch of government, 22–23

F
farming, 5, 7, 9, 27, 29–30
fishing, 5, 27
forests, 6, 12

G
garbage, disposal of, 8
garment industry, 27
Gilded Age, 17–18
Great Depression, 19

H
horses, for transportation and labor, 19
Hudson, Henry, 13
Hudson River, 6, 9

I
immigrants, 16, 18, 27

J
judicial branch of government, 25

L
legislative branch of government, 23–25
Long Island, 5, 9, 11, 14, 27
lowlands, 7–8

M
manufacturing industry, 26–27, 29
Morgan, John Pierpont, 17
mountains, 6–7

N
Native Americans, 13, 15, 34
New Amsterdam, 14
New York City, 5, 8, 11, 14–15, 16, 17–18, 20
  boroughs of, 10, 11, 18
  entertainment in, 5
  famous landmarks in, 10
  jobs in, 16, 26–27
  as nation's capital, 15, 21
  as state capital, 21
  tourism in, 28
New York State
  climate of, 8, 11
  economy of, 26–30
  famous people from, 31–36

Index

geography/regions of, 6–10
government of, 21–25
history of, 13–20
industry in, 16, 17, 19
variety of life in, 5
Niagara Falls, 9, 28
North Country, 6–7, 11, 12

P

Paleo-Indians, 13
plants, 11, 12
pollution, 8
publishing industry, 27

R

Revolutionary War, 14–15, 18
Rochester, 11, 27
Rockefeller, John D., 17
Roosevelt, Franklin Delano, 19, 23
Roosevelt, Theodore, 18, 19, 23

S

September 11 terrorist attacks, 20
service-related industry, 26, 27
slavery, 16
sporting events, 5, 11
Statue of Liberty, 10, 18, 34
stock market crash, 19
Syracuse, 11

T

Tammany Hall, 18
tourism, 9, 26, 28
Tweed, William Marcy "Boss," 18

V

valleys, 7–9
Van Buren, Martin, 23
Vanderbilt, Cornelius, 17
Verrazano, Giovanni da, 13
vineyards, 9, 29
voting, history of, 24

W

Washington, George, 14–15
World Trade Center, 20

NEW YORK: Past and Present

About the Author

J. Elizabeth Mills worked in Manhattan for eight years as a children's book editor. She now lives in Seattle, Washington, and writes nonfiction for young adults. She travels back to New York as often as possible!

Photo Credits

Cover (top left), p. 23 Library of Congress Prints and Photographs Division; cover (top right) Ramin Talaie/Getty Images; cover (bottom) © www.istockphoto.com/Jill Lang; pp. 3, 6, 13, 21, 26, 31, 37, 39 (left) Shutterstock.com; p. 4 (top) © GeoAtlas; p. 7 Yves Marcoux/First Light/Getty Images; p. 10 © www.istockphoto.com/Adam Kazmierski; p. 12 © Annie Griffiths Belt/Corbis; pp. 14, 15, 17 The New York Public Library/Art Resource, NY; p. 20 Archive Holdings, Inc./Hulton Archive/Getty Images; p. 22 © Lake County Museum/Corbis; p. 25 Wikipedia; p. 27 Emmanuel Aguirre/Getty Images; p. 28 © Ralf-Finn Hestoft/Corbis; p. 29 © Joey Nigh/Corbis; p. 32 Paul J. Richards/AFP/Getty Images; p. 33 Jeff Haynes/AFP/Getty Images; pp. 36, 39 (right) Wikimedia Commons; p. 38 (left) Courtesy of Robesus, Inc.

Designer: Les Kanturek; Editor: Bethany Bryan;
Photo Researcher: Amy Feinberg